Heart Tones

Daniel S. Terry

Song Lyrics and Music, 2017-2021

Heart Tones is published by Unfolding Communications
P.O. Box 57234
Lincoln, NE 68505
www.UnfoldingCommunications.com

Ebook ISBN: 978-1-7374354-1-9
Paperback ISBN: 978-1-7374354-0-2
Cover design by Nichole Hansen
Photography by Daniel S. Terry
Edited by Linda Stephen

Lyrics and Music by Daniel S. Terry

Songwriter web site: DanielSTerrySongs.com

DEDICATION

To my children whom I adore and love dearly, Josh and Caley. They have listened to many a new song over and over and over again. To my brothers and sisters who kindly put up with my attempts at rhymes over the years.

Heart Tones

Contents

Move On: Songs of Early 2021 1

  Move On.. 1

  In My Arms 3

Every Saint: Songs of 2020 6

  It's Gonna Get Better 6

  Can Love Grab Hold... 9

  How Do You Get 11

  The Girl from Jericho.. 13

  Don't Light the Torch.. 15

  The Human Heart 17

  Big City Lights.. 19

  I've Got a Plan for Heaven.. 21

  Heads or Tails.. 23

  Summer's Here... 25

  Gold Digger.. 27

  Through the Glass 29

  Every Saint 31

  Grateful for Love 33

  Every Storm... 35

Heart Tones: Songs of 2019 37

  Heart Tones 37

  My Life Is Better with You... 39

  She Couldn't Remember 41

  Who's Got Your Back... 43

Can't Stop, Won't Stop 45

Out of Time 47

The Sky Is Crying 49

Widow of the Oceans 51

My Dad 53

The Only Way Is Up 55

There's a New Day Coming 56

A Woman in His Life: Songs of 2018 59

When She Loves 59

A Woman in His Life 62

Which Way to Go 63

Mistress 65

Take a Chance on Our Dance 67

Diamond in the Rough 69

Enough of This Fight 71

Who's Going to Sing to You? 73

There's Time for That 75

Leaping into Heaven 77

To the Night 79

What's It Going to Take? 81

I'll Never Be the Same 83

The Sun Rises 85

Can He Care? 87

Hop a Plane 89

Driving in a Whiteout 91

I Got on a Plane: Songs of 2017 94

Island Christmas 94

Whiskey Is Warm 97

I'll Never Stop Falling in Love 99

The Day You Were Born 101

Cassini Bound.. 103

If I Could Walk Away... 105

A Song for Susan... 107

I Had Two Mothers.. 109

I Got on a Plane.. 111

What He'd Do for You... 113

Raw Sugar... 115

Leave Your Love Behind.. 117

Met This Woman... 119

The American Dream... 121

About the Songwriter 123

Index... 124

Alphabetical Listing of Songs.................... 128

Acknowledgements

Songwriting is a personal journey that you share with others. This book is dedicated to all the wonderful people in my life over the years who gave me encouragement, feedback, advice, and criticism on my music.

My creative journey started at the age of eight, when I began to write poetry and sing in church. Being from a large family, I needed to find a way to express myself in a personal manner. When I was nine, my cousin Tim Terry came on vacation with my family and brought his guitar. I still remember him singing "Michael, Row the Boat Ashore." The following year, my older sister Peggie had a party and someone left a guitar. I rescued it, bought a tuning fork and a Beatles book and taught myself how to play. Within two years, my mom died unexpectedly, and I started writing music.

Heart Tones: Song Lyrics & Music, 2017-2021 is a book of the 60-some odd songs that I have written from 2017 to early 2021.

This book started after a friend, someone nominated for a Grammy, told me I should publish a book of my lyrics. I told her that my gift was melody and composition, but she insisted that I was a lyricist. *Heart Tones* is the result of a very persistent friend.

I am especially thankful for my friend Marc Beeson, who helped me with my early attempts at songwriting after my mom died, and for the fantastic advice, after my divorce, of song coach Steve Leslie, my brother from another mother.

Thank you, also, to my editor Linda Stephen for all her guidance and advice. *Heart Tones* would not have happened without her.

Over the years, music has been a way for me to create and express myself – and hopefully improve the world in just a little way. Thank you to all who have supported me on my songwriting journey. Life is good!

Move On: Songs of Early 2021

"Move On" was my 50th professionally recorded song in Nashville.
Thank you to co-writer Rebecca TenBrink. We've all been in those
relationships where it was just time to go.

Move On
March 28, 2021
Written with Rebecca TenBrink

Chorus:
(and, but) He's like a fish out of water just a lump on a log
without her
Just a deer caught in the headlights
But girl you gotta move on, time to be long gone
Move on, time to live your life
Move on, gotta end that strife
Move on

He's had a breakthrough, Pit stop clear view
But her fresh start, her redo
Will let her stop the damage

Chorus

1

He didn't think she'd do well
But she chose to shine, first in line
Double time

Chorus

Bridge

She never thought he'd be so jealous
and so controlling

Chorus

She has a new job, she buys nice things
Doesn't care about that damn diamond ring
or his little things

Chorus

Chords:
Key of B
Em7 Cadd9 Em7 Cadd9
Am F#m7#5 Am F#m7#5
Chorus:
G F#m7#5 Em C B
G F#m7#5 Em C B
Am F#m7#5 Am F#m7#5
G F#m7#5 Em C B
G F#m7#5 Em C B
Bridge:
Em Bm C F#m7#5

In My Arms
January 29, 2021

I opened the door, smelled her perfume
and I wanted more, wanted more
She glided across, never touching ground
She's just an angel that's earthly bound

Chorus:
How could this be true
Or am I just a fool
Will this love be cruel?
But hey, it's just too hard to believe
why she wants a devil like me.
When will she be in my arms again?

Who would have thought
She blew across that open field
into my open arms

Chorus

Bridge

In my arms, oh, in my arms,
Oh, in my arms again

In my arms, oh, in my arms,
Oh, in my arms again

Chorus

How my heart explodes
I'll grab ahold
of this angel
And not let go

Chorus

I opened the door, smelled her perfume
and I wanted more, wanted more
She glided across, never touching ground
She's just an angel that's earthly bound

Chorus

Chords:
Capo II Key of A
G Am7 Am7/C G
G Am7 Am7/C G
G Am7 Am7/C Em G
G Am7 Am7/C G
G Am7 Am7/C G
G Am7 Am7/C Em G
Chorus:
F G Am7
F G Em
F G Am7 Am7/C
F Am7
F Am7
F Am7
Bridge:
G F Em Am
G F Em Am

Heart Tones

Every Saint: Songs of 2020

2020 was a very productive year musically for me. I only recorded seven songs in Nashville but had eight music videos made, and wrote many new songs, which have since been recorded in Nashville, Tennessee and Roanoke, Virginia.

Before the pandemic, I went through a marriage break up. For most of 2020, I was suddenly working from home. It was a great time for making music and playing outside at local parks. Some of my favorite songs: "Summer's Here," "How Do You Get," and "Through the Glass."

It's Gonna Get Better
December 27, 2020

I couldn't make this up
Couldn't have written the script
The times we are living in
can make our heart flip

Chorus:
When your heart flips, it skips

It knows when it's sick
And we all know
Oh, we all know
it's gonna get better

She wouldn't take my hand,
She just walked away
The heart as a leader
will make it okay

Chorus
And we all know
Oh, we all know
it's gonna get better

Love will come
and love can be a no show
The heart as a soldier
can help your soul

Chorus

And we all know
Oh, we all know
it's gonna get better
The heart as a leader
will make it okay

Chorus

I couldn't make this up
Couldn't have written the script
The times we are living in
can make our heart flip

Chorus

And we all know
Oh, we all know
it's gonna get better

Chords:
Capo II Key of A
G F#m#5 Em C
G F#m#5 Em C
G F#m#5 Em C
G F#m#5 Em C
Chorus:
Am Gmaj Cadd7
Am Gmaj Cadd7

Can Love Grab Hold
November 26, 2020

How could she be so cute
How could she be so kind
How could you be that lady who's on his mind

Chorus:
Seasons come and seasons go, can love grab hold
Leaves will fall and snow will blow, can love grab hold

How could she be so tough
How could she be so fun
How could she be the lady that's hotter than the sun

Chorus

Lead

Chorus

Bridge

She thinks it's true, she wants to get to know him, know him
She knows it's true, she's gonna find some time with him

Chorus

How could she be so wise
How could she be so smart
How could she be that lady
Who's captured his heart

Chorus

How could she be so cute
How could she be so kind
How could she be that lady who's always on his mind

Chorus

Chords:
Capo II Key of E
D6 C G
D6 C G
D6 C Am7 Am7 Em
Chorus:
F G Em Am7 F G
F G Em

How Do You Get
November 1, 2020

Chorus:
How do you get, how do you get
a love like that?
How do you get, how do you get
a love like that?
Who do you know,
where do you go for that?
How do you find, do you stand in line for that?

I'm looking for love, looking for that life
My friends say hey, hey, hey
you need a wife
I tried that twice. Didn't work out
Not sure who's at fault

Chorus

I went to church, I searched the mall
I asked my aunt, do you know anyone at all?
But I struck out it seems
No girl of my dreams

Chorus

I took a cruise
They said you couldn't lose
Salt water and bathing suits.
But I struck out.
Rough seas, spent time on my knees

Chorus

I went to work, I went to church
Took a cruise some felt you couldn't lose
but I struck out it seems
No girl of my dreams

Chorus

Chords:
Capo II Key of E
D5 Bm7 A D5 Bm7 A
D5 Bm7 A B5 A5/E B5 A5/E
Chorus:
Bm A G F#m#5 A7 A
Bm A G F#m#5 A7 A
Em F#m#5 G A7 A
Em F

The Girl from Jericho

October 17, 2020
Written with Emily Zuzelski

He found the letter tucked in the book
he put there long ago
A note from a lover
someone he cherished
but he had to let her go

Chorus:
How many years of lonely nights
How many tears can he cry
How can he find that girl he loved
The girl he left behind
She lived on Jericho, the street down the road
That girl from Jericho, the one he used to know
That girl from Jericho

She liked to cycle, so did he
They met on that trail
She was fearless, so much quicker
In a race he failed

Chorus

Lead

Bridge

He wasn't old enough, mature enough to know
The love she gave him was pure as driven snow
That girl from Jericho
Jericho, Jericho, Jericho, Jericho, Jericho, Jericho

Chorus

He hopped on his bike
and took the path just to clear his mind
She was out riding
with one of her kids
and her son waved hi

Chorus

Jericho, Jericho, Jericho, Jericho
Jericho, Jericho, Jericho

Chords:
Capo I Key of C#
C Cadd4 C Cadd4 C Cadd4 G
C Cadd4 C Cadd4 C Cadd4 G
Chorus:
Am Em F G
Am Em F
Am Em F G
F G
Em F C G
Em F C G
C G
Bridge:
Am Em F G
Am Em F G

Don't Light the Torch
September 29, 2020
Written with Emily Zuzelski

I've been sitting behind this wheel
five hours and then some
Just a few more to go
I don't know how I'm going to feel
going home's just a bit too real
I made it home to my folks
Boy, how they have aged
There's decisions to be made
I don't know how I'm going to feel
Going home's just a bit too real

Chorus:
Don't light the torch if you can't stand the heat
Love and care is a two-lane street
Don't light the torch, don't light the torch
Don't light the torch
if you can't stand the heat, can't stand the heat
Don't light that torch, don't light that torch

I never thought that my folks'd grow old
Mom's memory has gone
Dad's still getting around
I don't know how I'm going to feel
Going home's just a bit too real
I don't know how I'm going to feel

Chorus

Lead

Chorus

I've been sitting behind this wheel
five hours and then some

Just a few more to go
I don't know how I'm going to feel
Going home's just a bit too real

Chorus

I don't know how I'm going to feel
Going home's just a bit too real
I don't know how I'm going to feel

Chords:
Capo I Key of G#
G F#m#5 Am
G F#m#5 Am
G F#m#5 Am
Em B7 Em G
Em B7 Em G
Chorus:
D G Em Bm
D G Em Bm
C CM7/B Am7 Am7/G
C CM7/B Am7 Am7/G
C CM7/B Am7 Am7/G
G B7 Em C
G B7 Em C
G B7 Em C

The Human Heart

September 11, 2020
Written with Emily Zuzelski

What a year that it's been
Can't forget this one
Hearts are breaking, souls were takin'
We've got work to be done
We can smile and choose to be kind
It doesn't cost you a dime
Give some joy, a song or a laugh
Simply give someone your time

Chorus:
It's the mystery of the human heart
of how much it can love
The more you give
the more you get back
of the human heart

You choose your attitude when you wake
It smooths out the waves
Not like the boat that pushes back
and struggles in its wake

Give some joy, a song, or a laugh
Simply give someone your time

Chorus 2:
Oh, the mystery of the human heart
of how much it can love
The more you give,
the more you get back
of the human heart

Solo:
We can smile and choose to be kind
It doesn't cost you a dime

Give some joy, a song, or a laugh
Simply give someone your time

Chorus 3:
Oh, the mystery of the human heart
of how much it can love
The more you give
the more you get back
of the human heart

Oh, the music of the human heart
of how much it can love
The more you give
the more you get back
of the human heart

Chords:
Capo II Key of D
FM9/E Am7/E FM9/E Am7/E
FM9/E Am7/E
Gsus2sus4 G Gsus2sus4 G
FM9/E Am7/E FM9/E Am7/E
FM9/E Am7/E
Gsus2sus4 G Gsus2sus4 G
Em F G C Am
Em F G C Am
Chorus:
G F C Am
G F C
G F C Am G

Big City Lights
August 17, 2020

He has a hole in his heart
something's missing
He doesn't know what to do
'cause it's not working
No matter how he tries
she can't hide

She needs her job and friends
that's what she's missin'
He doesn't want her to go
he'll miss her kissin'
no matter how he tries
she can't hide

Chorus:
She's gotta go back and live her life
It's not her fault she needs those big city lights
She's gotta go back, gotta go back, gotta go back
to big city lights
to big city lights

Through the subways and the elevators
All those buildings and tall skyscrapers
no matter how she tries
she can't hide

Chorus

Solo:
She has a hole in her heart
He can't fix it
She wants her life back
And he's not in it
No matter how he tries
she can't hide

Chorus

He has a hole in his heart
something missing
He doesn't know what to do
it's not worth fixing
No matter how he tries
She can't hide

Chorus

Chords:
Capo II Key of D
Am G Fmaj7
Am G Fmaj7
Em Fmaj7
Em Fadd9
Chorus:
Dm G C B Am G
Dm G C B Am G
Fmaj7 Fmaj#11sus2 Fmaj7 Fmaj#11sus2

I've Got a Plan for Heaven
August 2, 2020

I'll love you 'til eternity and one day more
We had our walk with destiny
when you came through that door
We couldn't know, how the night would end
We didn't know how we'd feel

Chorus:
I've got a plan for heaven
I've got a plan for heaven with you
with you, with you, with you

We live in such crazy times,
and you gotta keep your distance
No shaking hands, no hugs or kisses
I miss my kids, my family, my friends, and my loves
But mostly I miss you

Chorus

Lead

I miss my kids, my family, my friends, and my loves
But mostly I miss you

Chorus 2:
I've got a plan for heaven
I've got a plan for heaven
I've got a plan for heaven with you
with you, with you, with you

Life is the flower, love is the honey
When you have it, it's more important than money
I miss my kids, my friends, my family, and my loves
But I mostly miss you

Chorus 3:
I've got a plan for heaven
I've got a plan for heaven
I've got a plan for heaven with you
with you, with you, with you
with you, with you, with you

Chords:
Key of E
E G#9add5addb13 A F#7#9sus4
E G#9add5addb13 A B
A G#9add5addb13 G#mMb13 C#m7 C#m7/G#
A G#9add5addb13 G#mMb13
Chorus:
F#7#9sus4 G#9add5addb13 A B
F#7#9sus4 G#9add5addb13 A B
E G#9add5addb13 A B
E G#9add5addb13 A B

Heads or Tails
July 20, 2020

They met in high school,
such a perfect pair always together
They both loved horses, how they'd ride side by side

Chorus:
She's going to flip that coin
Is it heads or tails, heads or tail
She's got to leave this town
Is it north or south, north or south
What heals you best, is it east or west, east or west
She just knows she has to go
Heads or tails, heads or tails

They didn't date till junior year that's what Dad said
They had to wait, school and sports kept her safe

Chorus

Though they wed, it didn't last, love fell flat
Now she knows, he slept around, wasn't picky

Break

She needs to love again
Find a man, throw fate to the wind
throw fate to the wind

Chorus

So, she packed those bags, filled her tank, headed out
When she arrived, it felt like home, she walked about

Chorus

Chords:

Capo II Key of E

Dm F6 Em7 Cadd9

Dm F6 Em7 Cadd9

Dm F6 Em7 Cadd9

Chorus:

Am F G

Am F G

Am F G

Em F C G

Summer's Here
July 12, 2020

Summer's here, let's head to the beach
the waves are crashing down
and the wind keeps blowing sand around

Summer's here, let's break out those suits
the sun is sitting high and hot
the nighttime sky stars are out

Chorus:
Hey, hey, let's go out 'cause
Summer's here
Hey, hey, let's get out 'cause
Girl, summer's finally here

Summer's here, let's drive to the woods
they've got plenty of trails to hike
We can even bring our bikes

Summer's here, let's walk to the park
Bring your picnic basket
and I'll bring my guitar

Chorus

Lead

Chorus

Break

And the winter was so cruel to us
The snow and ice piled high
But winter's over girl for us

Summer's here, let's ride to the lake
the fish are big and strong
and all we've got to do is hook 'em on, oh

Summer's here, let's walk to the park
Bring your picnic basket
and I'll bring my guitar

Chorus

Summer's here, let's head to the beach
the waves are crashing down
and the wind keeps blowing sand around

Summer's here, let's break out those suits
the sun is sitting high and hot
the nighttime sky stars are out

Chorus

Chorus

Chords:
Capo II Key of D
C G Am Em
F G F G
C G Am Em
F G F G
Chorus:
F G Em Am
F G Am
F G Em Am
F F G
Break:
F Em Am G
F Em Am Am
F Em Am G

Gold Digger
June 7, 2020

I used to think she loved me
I used to think she cared
But dollar signs showed up
so buyer beware
Dollar signs showed up
so buyer beware

Today turns into tomorrow
none too soon
It's time to move on
I'm gonna shoot the moon
Time to move on
I'm gonna shoot the moon

Chorus:
She's a heart breakin', soul takin', gold diggin' girl
She's a show stopper, bank robber, gold diggin' girl

Chorus

Comets come and comets go
They know their way
My compass's been broken
Please get it replaced
My compass's been broken
Come, please replace

Chorus

She'll take your heart
Take your soul
Take your everything you own
I don't deal with liars
Don't know their kind
But she keeps spinning

that same old lie
She keeps spinning
that same old line

Chorus

I used to think she loved me
I used to think she cared
But dollar signs showed up
so buyer beware
Dollar signs showed up
so buyer beware

Chorus

Chorus

Chorus

Chords:
Capo II
Dsus4 Em C G B7 Em C G
Dsus4 Em C G B7 Em C G
B7 Em C G
Chorus:
Am Bm Cadd9 G
Am Bm Cadd9 G
Bridge:
Am Bm Am Bm Am Bm G

Through the Glass
May 4, 2020

The light comes streaming in
As it hits the glass
It shows two pairs of palm prints
That's all that's left
They packed that truck in the morning
and left town
I come back from work
and they're gone

Chorus:
I know I don't have
a soul of a saint
I know I made mistakes
But this too in time will pass
As I sit here and look through the glass

You gotta take some risks
to get ahead
Life and love aren't different
they share the same bed
You just got to find that love
no matter where it goes
It might be right beside you
or across the globe

Chorus

Lead

Chorus

The light comes streaming in
as it hits the glass
It shows two pairs of palm prints
That's all that's left

Chorus

Chorus

Chords:
Capo II Key of D
C Am C Am
C Am C Am
C Am C Am
F G
C Am C Am
C Am C Am
C Am C Am
F G
Chorus:
F G C
F G Am
F G C
F G

Every Saint
April 26, 2020

They used to be lovers, walked the beach
holding hands, crunching the sand
They used to go out riding, hit the trails
and viewed life atop a horse
swaying off course

Chorus 1:
Every saint has a past
Every sinner a future
What will survive us,
is our love for each other,
girl, our love

They broke up and went
their ways
Not sure what happened
It just happened
They went their ways

Chorus 2:
Every saint has his past
Every sinner his future
What will survive us,
is our love girl,
oh, our love

Lead

Chorus 1

Break

He knew that you were right for him
He wants his life soon to begin

He's looking for you

*Choru*s 1

They met online after all those years
The spark glowed and it roared
The spark did roar

Chorus 1

They went out walking

Chords:
Capo I Key of D#
D DM7sus2 D6 DM7sus2 D
D DM7sus2 D6 DM7sus2 D
A A7sus4add6 A7omit 3 A7sus4add6 A
D DM7sus2 D6 DM7sus2 D
Chorus:
Bm F#m11 F#m7#5 Em A
Bm F#m11 F#m7#5 Em A
Break:
G F#m7#5 A
G F#m7#5 A

Grateful for Love
April 12, 2020

I've been given too much, or so it seems
I am grateful, and there's no in betweens
I'm just happy to sing a song or two
Sit on down, and I'll play a few

It's a good day when a song shows up
My heart explodes, and I can't get enough
It's a wacky life we all live
I'm just happy to be here
and happy to give

Chorus:
Sing a song, sing of life, sing of love
Sing for babies, and springtime and stars above
Sing a song, sing of life, sing of love
I am grateful for you, and I'm grateful for love
I'm grateful for love

It's the glue that holds us tight
It's what matters deep at night
It's the mother that holds her child
It's the father who goes mile after mile

Chorus

I've been given too much, from above
I am grateful, and I am loved
It's a good day when a song shows up
My heart explodes, and I can't get enough

Chorus

I'm grateful for you
I'm grateful for love

Chords:

Capo II Key of A

G F#m7#5 Em C

Am Bm Cadd9

G F#m7#5 Em C

Am Bm Cadd9

Chorus:

Em F#m7#5 C G

Em F#m7#5 C G Am Bm Cadd9

Every Storm
February 2, 2020

I am just a man, just a guy
who's headed out that door
I am just a man, just a guy
Won't take it no more

Chorus 1:
Cause every storm runs out of rain
every witness has their say
every heart wants to love
one day

How could it happen twice, you were so kind
But you've had your say, and I've had mine

I'm going to be that guy
who heads out that door
I'm going to be that guy
who won't take it no more

Chorus 2
Cause every mountain's got a view
Every window's got its pane
Every heart wants to love one day

Lead

I am just a man, just a guy
who's headed out that door
I am just a man, just a guy
won't take it no more

Chorus 1

We thought it was true love
but it didn't turn out that way

So I'm going to be that guy
who heads out that door
I'm going to be that guy
who won't take it no more

Chorus 1

I am just a man, just a guy
who's headed out that door
I am just a man, just a guy
Won't take it no more

Chorus 2

Chords:
Capo II Key of A
G walkup C G/Bmaj Am7 Em/G F#m7#5
G walkup C G/Bmaj Am7 Em/G F#m7#5

Heart Tones: Songs of 2019

2019 marked my first professional music video with Alexandra Sedlak and GOLDFOX LLC Video. It was an eventful year musically: I recorded 21 songs in Nashville, Tennessee and 10 at Skip Brown's Final Track Studios in Roanoke, Virginia. Some of my most moving songs: "She Couldn't Remember," "Heart Tones," "Widow of the Ocean" and "The Only Way Is Up." It is always a good day when a song shows up.

Heart Tones
December 31, 2019

The cask is half full of brew
been years in waiting, just for you
Steep a little more, brew a little more
I'll tap this cask and think of love
Just to savor my girl from above, girl from above
Brew a little more

Chorus:
The sky is turning black
you're still smiling like the sun is shining
there's no turning back

We committed
our hearts submitted
I'll follow you thru different time zones
My heart tones ring true, ring true
My heart tones my heart tones ring true

I've been so thankful for you in my life
You've got that knack of turning night bright
Brew a little more, brew a little more

Bridge

I'll do anything I can to be with you
I'll give all my love to no one but you,
to no one but you

Lead

Chorus

Chords:
Capo II Key of D
C Am7 C Bm Am7 Am7/G
C Am7 C Bm Am7 Bm Am7 Am7/G
Fmaj7 Fmaj7 C G
Fmaj7 Fmaj7 C G
Chorus:
Am Em F G
Am Em F G
Am Em F G
C Em F G
Bridge:
Em F C G
Em F C G

My Life Is Better with You
November 23, 2019

The sun is crawling up in an hour
Let's get out of bed and greet it
You know how the sun can peel back the darkness
and fill our days with
light and warmth and gets a little hotter
with you by my side

Chorus:
My life is better with you in it
We have such crazy fun
My life is better with you in it
So darling let's go and greet the sun/moon

As it burns off the morning mist, it's going to be a great day
and you turn and give me a kiss, it's all I can say
cause there's light and warmth, and gets a little hotter
with you by my side

Chorus

Lead:
And there's warmth and gets a little hotter
with you by my side

Chorus (moon)

As it shines through the darkness, playing tag with the clouds
And I know that it has many faces
some slivers of and slivers of
light and not much warmth and gets a little hotter
with you by my side

Chorus

Chorus

Chords:

No capo Key of A

A C#M F#m Bm E

A C#m F#m Bm E

Chorus:

Bm C#m D E

D E A F#m Bm E

D E A F#m Bm E

She Couldn't Remember
October 23, 2019

She couldn't remember the name of her husband
or the 50 years of life and love

Chorus:
The windows broken,
light can't get thru
But she (he) still remembers you

She couldn't remember the birthdays of her children
or the laughs or looks

Chorus

Break

Chorus

Bridge:
He remembers all the good times, not the bad
He'll stand by you with every breath he has
every breath

He still remembers the day that they met
The wind was blowing
Her hair was a mess

Chorus

He still remembers you

She couldn't remember the day that they wed
Nor the dress or the flowers that she threw

Chorus

She couldn't remember the name
of her husband
or the 50 years of life and love

Chorus

He still remembers you
He still remembers you

Chords:
Capo II Key of B
Intro
A C#m7 D E
A C#m7 D E
A C#m7 D E
Chorus:
D E A G# F#m
D E F#m
Bridge:
C#m7 F#m D A
C#m7 F#m D A

Who's Got Your Back
October 13, 2019

Who's got your back, who's got your front
Who can tell the truth, who can be blunt
You know you need to work on this
You think it should be me
You think it should be me

Chorus:
You want us to be lovers
I want to be that guy
When we talk with each other
I know and you know that it shows
I'll be your guy

I got your back, I got your front
I'll keep you safe, and I'll be blunt
You know you need some help with this
You think it should be me
You think it should be me

Chorus

Lead:
You know you need some help with this
You think it should be me

Chorus

Break

It's a match made in heaven
It's a match of love
It's a life we're living
You know that it shows, and I know
I'll be your guy
I'll be your guy

Who's got your back, who's got your front
Who can tell the truth, who can be blunt
You know you need some help with this
You think it should be me
I think it should be me

Chorus

I've got your back, I've got your front

Chords:
Capo II Key of F#
Em C D G
Em C D G
Em C D G
Bm C Bm C
Chorus:
D G Em Bm
D G Am B C
Break:
Bm Em D G
Bm Em Am Bm7 C

Can't Stop, Won't Stop
September 29, 2019

The bees gotta build their hives and those ants dig in the earth
I was lost till you found me, kept my feet on top of the dirt

Pre-chorus:
How do the robins know where to go, before the cold and snow
and you know, you do, you know that it's true

Chorus:
That I can't stop won't stop loving you
(Birds wanna sing and those birds do ring)
Hearts want to dance looking for true romance,
'Cause I can't stop, won't stop loving you
'Cause I can't stop, won't stop loving you

I never thought it could happen
That love could find me twice
But when I did meet you, I knew your looks could melt my ice

Pre-chorus

Chorus

Break

Pre-chorus

Chorus

Chords:

Capo I Key F

E F#m A E

E F#m A E

Chorus:

A G# F#m E

A G# F#m E

F#m Bm G#m A B

C#m G#m

A B A B

C#m G#m

A B A B

E F#m A E

Out of Time
September 15, 2019

We keep running out of time
The sun comes up too quick
You keep driving me out of my mind,
and my heart skips a bit
Nothing is easy
Life can be crazy
You got your projects,
and I love my job
Distance and commitments
make it hard
Nothing is easy
Life can be crazy

Chorus:
We're out of time
so much fills our day
We're out of time
so much gets in our way
I just want you today

Seasons come and seasons go,
and I'll stay the same.
The magic that we have
is sure to blame.
Nothing is easy
Life can be crazy

Chorus

We keep running out of time
The moon sets so fast
With you in my arms
let's make the moment last
Nothing is easy
Life can be crazy

Chorus

Chords:
Capo IV
Em C D/F#maj
Em C D/F#maj
Em C D/F#maj
Em C D/F#maj
Bm7 C
Bm7 C
Chorus:
Am D/F#maj G F# Em
Am D/F#maj G F# Em
Am

The Sky Is Crying
September 5, 2019

The storms across the lake
come hard and fast
The clouds are tall,
and angry and black

Chorus:
The sky is crying, and you are in my arms
There's nothing better than the time that we call ours
And the rain keeps hammerin' down
And your heart and my heart do pound

Whitecaps are crashing
against the shore
The wind is whipping
against your door

Chorus

Lead

Our love gets stronger with each
crashing wave
Though the light show and
the thunder is for the brave
And the rain keeps hammering down
and your heart and my heart do pound

Chorus

Break

Whitecaps are crashing
against the shore
The wind keeps whipping
against your door

Chorus

And your heart and my heart do pound
And your heart and my heart do pound
And your heart and my heart do pound

Chords:
Capo IV
Am Em7 Am Em7
Am Em7 Am Em7
Chorus:
D5 C G F#m#5
D5 C G F#m#5
Em C F#m#5
Em C F#m#5
Break:
Bm Cadd9 Em F#m#5
Bm Cadd9 Em F#m#5

Widow of the Oceans
July 1, 2019

She gets up from her chair
Looks 'cross the bay
and wonders where the time went
wonders where the time went
It started when she was young
Fell in love with a man who loved the sea
Wondered where the time went

Chorus:
She's a widow of the oceans
she's a widow of the seas
she's a widow of tomorrows
with wishes that could be
she's a widow of the water
that she seems to know
wondering when her man/love will come home

We're just a bit like her
by the window hoping our love comes home
hoping our love comes home

Chorus

Break

Chorus

We wish that we could help
The heart's a force that's
tough to deal with
Wondering where the time went

Chorus

Chorus

Chords:

Capo II Key of A

G F#mb5 Asus4 C D

Em C G F@mb5 G

G F#mb5 Asus4 C D

Em C G F@mb5 G

Chorus:

Em Bm C G

Em Bm C D

Em Bm C G Am D G

My Dad
June 9, 2019

I've been thinking about my dad
He was a man of many talents
He could hit that tennis ball
He took the net, he was ruthless

Chorus:
What's a son to do, when he misses his dad
I/You can't turn back time, I/You want to
I/You can't roll back time, I/You wish to
I/You can't bring him back, but I/you can miss him,
you can miss him so

He was the father of eight, a crazy crew,
his own tribe
They'd stuff us into that wagon
long before seat belts

Chorus

Break

How could it happen
that you became him
And how could you care about the color
of your your – Wooooo
He was a country doc
he still made house calls on the weekends
so many babies delivered
All of those lives in his hands

Chorus

I've been thinking about my dad

Chords:

Capo IV Key of F#

D5 Em11 GM7sus/A D5add flat 9 Dm7sus2 add 6

D5 Em11 GM7sus/A D5add flat 9 Dm7sus2 add 6

D5 Em11 GM7sus/A D5add flat 9 Dm7sus2 add 6

Chorus:

B C# D5 Em add 9 Em bb5

D5 B A

D5 B A

D5 B A

Em add 9 A/E 5th

Break:

Bm A G

Bm A G

Bm A G F#/D A7

The Only Way Is Up
January 27, 2019

She cries out and fights back those tears
It's been rough, for too many years, too many years

Chorus:
What's a single mom to do alone
when her luck has run out
and the winds that blow seem to knock her down
and the only way is up?

She holds a child and looks into their eyes
and sees the love, the love that helps her thrive
helps her thrive

Chorus

She closes her eyes and dreams of better times
knows the why and the hill she needs to climb,
needs to climb

Chorus

Chords:
Capo IV Key of Db or C#
C#m#5/E Esus4 C#m7/E C#m7/G#
D6sus2 D6sus2/A
C#m#5/E Esus4 C#m7/E C#m7/G#
D6sus2 D6sus2/A D6sus2 D6sus2/A
Chorus:
D E A F#m11
D E F#m11
D E A F#m11
D E F#m11

There's a New Day Coming
January 13, 2019

I got a call today.
A friend of mine has died.
We used to sing together.
Why, oh why, oh why?

He burned the candle at both ends
It ran a little hot
Life can be nutty
Or maybe not

Chorus:
But who's got time to grieve
I'll wipe my tears on my sleeve
Cause there's a new day coming
I'll be up and running
So, wipe your eyes and bring your smile
tomorrow, tomorrow

Some friends will be with you
and others leave too soon
Just raise a glass to toast them
and wish they were in the room

Chorus

Life can be precious
Life can be dear
So, grab ahold with both hands
and remain here

Chorus

Hold your breath and deal with death tomorrow
Wipe your eyes and bring your smile tomorrow
So, wipe your tears and leave your fears tomorrow
Come hold my hand, and I'll be a man tomorrow
Close your eyes lady
The sun has lost its place
night has taken over
time to pull the shade

Chorus

We've been working too long
You've been painting, and I'm on that song

There's a new day coming
We've been off and running
So, close your eyes, but bring your smile
tomorrow, tomorrow

Get some sleep my lady

Chords:
Capo I Key of D#
D B
Chorus:
Bm F#m G6
Bm F#m G6
Em F#m G6

Heart Tones

A Woman in His Life: Songs of 2018

2018 was an eventful year for me, traveling twice a month to England to date, writing music at airport gates in London, Chicago, Nashville, Florence, Rome, Monaco, and Italy's Lake Como. It was just a great year for creativity. "The Sun Rises," "To the Night," "A Woman in His Life," "Diamond in the Rough" and "Mistress" stand out as songs written on the road. Life is very good.

When She Loves
December 4, 2018
Miami

Chorus:
When she loves, she loves
and everyone knows
and when she gives, she gives
'til that old wind goes
down the road

'til young hearts explode

The clock on the wall tells the time
Every 12 hours it's right
She didn't think it would strike twice
but her head and heart found a way

Chorus

When they met, they could see
there was fire and heat
Now it's fun to go home
turn down your radio and phone

Chorus

Break

She needs to love, she needs to give,
she wants to know
is this man the one for her soul?
and can they grow old together?

Chorus

The clock on the wall tells the time
Two times a day it's right

Chorus

Chords:

Capo III Key of C
Amaj7 A6th Amaj7 A6th
Amaj7 A6th Amaj7 A6th
Bsus 2nd F#sus4th C#Em7 A/G#sus7 maj2
Amaj7 A6th Amaj7 A6th
Amaj7 A6th Amaj7 A6th
Bsus 2nd F#sus4th C#Em7 A/G#sus7 maj2
Chorus:
D E A G# F#m11
D E A G# F#m11
Bsus4 C#m7 G Bsus4 C#m7 G
Amaj7 A6th Amaj7 A6th
Amaj7 A6th Amaj7 A6th

A Woman in His Life
October 13, 2018

Another day with a smile on his face
no longer with an empty space
hasn't wanted to change his place

Chorus:
Walking through his seasons
Walking through his life
Everything has a reason
Cause there's a woman, oh there's a woman in his life

Sun comes up, and sun goes down
It's a honey day not a honeymoon
Time to get up but not too soon

Chorus

His house is full of laughter, and there's paintings everywhere
It's that ever after, cause there's a woman
Oh, there's a woman in his life

Chorus

Chords:
Capo III
G Am7/G G Am7/G
Em C Em C
G Am7/G G Am7/G
Chorus:
D Em C G
D Em C Am G Am7/G G Am7/G
Break:
Em C G Em C Am C G

Which Way to Go
August 30, 2018

He knows these girls
tiny toes and curls.
And when they sing
hearts beat and bees sting.
And when they dance and laugh
Life's given him a second chance.

Chorus:
Don't you know
that your heart
knows the road?
Your heart knows
which way to go.

(2nd and 3rd chorus)
Don't you feel
that this time is real.
Your heart steals a chance to know
which way to go
which way to go

He knows this life,
family, kids and wife.
It's what he's missed -
crazy days with goodnight kisses.
And when they dance and laugh,
life's given them a second chance.

Chorus

And when they dance and laugh,
life's given them a second chance.

Chorus

He knows these girls
tiny toes and curls

Chords:
Capo III Key of D
D B Asus4th D B Asus4th
D B Asus4th D B Asus4th
G F#m7#5th A A7 A A7
G F#m7#5th A A7 A A7
Chorus:
Bm A D5 G D5 G A A7

Mistress
August 3, 2018

She's dressed in the finest clothes
Been knocking on my door
I never know when she's going to show
Today or tomorrow
There's music in the air
When she's here
She could spend the night or be
gone in an hour

Chorus:
Music's my mistress
That I know
It's a good day when a song shows up, shows up
Music's my mistress
That I know
It's a good day when a song shows up, shows up

I keep hearing notes in my head
I need to connect them
There's a melody roaming around
Feelings linked with sound
You never know where
the song will go
such joy in the process
My soul does know

Chorus

Break

I love the last song
'til another one comes along

Chorus

Chords:

Capo III Key of D

Dsus2 C6add9 Bm11 D5/A

Bm11 C6 add9

Chorus:

Em11G Asus2 F#m11 Em11G

Em F#m11 Em11G

Take a Chance on Our Dance
July 29, 2018

How could I, how could I know?
I thought my heart was broke

Come with me, hold my hand tonight
Come with me and be my love
I've crossed the oceans just to be with you
Come with me, we'll greet the morning sun

How could I, how could I feel?
I thought you weren't real

Stay with me. I'll share my life with you.
Bring your loved ones, too.
Pack your bag, bring your paints and brush
Paint away, paint away with love (so)

Chorus:
Take a chance on our dance this year
The ballroom's open, and the floor is clear
I'll hold you tight and spin you around
Take a chance on our dance this year
and forever could be found

You saw, you saw the way
Through a foggy day
Be with me, I'll hold your heart so close
Be with me tonight
We've got laughter and joy in our hearts
Paint away, please paint away with love (and)

Chorus

Break

Chorus

Chords:
Capo III Key D
D5/C# D5/B D5/C# D5/B
A7 A G D
A7 A G D
A7 A G D
Bm G D G D A7
Chorus:
D5 Em D G
D5 Em D G
D5 Em D G
Bm7 A13 sup 4th Bm7 A13sus4th

Diamond in the Rough

June 9, 2018

She's an early spring
Just a little green
only seventeen
Just a little green

All the roads to choose
Which one will she use?
She's gotta wear those shoes
Which ones will she use?

Chorus:
She's a diamond in the rough
still a little tough
not sure if its love
but she shines

Come a little close
turn the light up high
you need to see those eyes
turn the light up high

Chorus

Chorus

Break

She gets up early just to go to work
stays late till the job is done
she's got that stuff, she's got that stuff

Chorus

Chorus

Chords:

Capo II C position

C G/B Am7 Am7/G

C G/B Am7   Am7/G

Fmaj7 FM#11 Fmaj7 FM#11

Fmaj7 FM#11 Fmaj7 FM#11

C G/B Am7 Am7/G

C G/B Am7   Am7/G

Fmaj7 FM#11 Fmaj7 FM#11

Fmaj7 FM#11 Fmaj7 FM#11

Enough of This Fight
April 28, 2018

He's had enough of this wife
20 years of his life
So many moments, good and bad
He's had enough of this wife

He's had enough of those eyes
Ocean blue-green lies
He could live without the truth
But he's had enough of those eyes

She took his guns and his pickup truck
His lucky coin and said good luck
She's changed the locks
and barred the door
She's barred the door

She's had enough of those lips
His strong and tender kiss
The song he'd sing on her way to work
But she's had enough of those lips

Chorus:
They've had enough of this fight
But not tonight
They'll hold each other like before
They've had enough of this fight

Chords:

Capo III Key G (Bb)
G F#m7#5 G
C Em7 D G
E C
G F#m7#5 G
G F#m7#5 G
C Em7 D G
E C
G F#m7#5 G
Chorus:
Am Em F G
Am F E7sus4 E7
Am Em F G
Am F E7sus4 E

Who's Going to Sing to You?

March 17, 2018
Florence, Italy

Who's going to sing to you on the day you die?
Who's going to hold you on that day?
Truth and justice is a mystery they say.
Wooo wooo

Will your friends remember what you said?
There was power in how you led.
Give them laughter and love instead.
Wooo wooo

Chorus:
You know you're just a man,
ashes to ashes and sand to sand.
You always broke those rules,
never thought you could lose,
always in search of the truth.

Who's going to kiss you on the day that you die?
Who's going to hold your hand?
Are your loved ones on the other side?
Wooo wooo

Chorus

Who's going to whisper those sweet lies on the day that you die?
Are there angels on the other side?
Wooo wooo

Chorus

Who's going to love you on the day that you die?

Who's going to hold your heart?
Are your loved ones going to sit and cry?
Wooo wooo
Chorus

Who's going to kiss you on the day you die?
Who's going to hold my heart?
Who'll miss me on the other side?
Wooo wooo

Chorus

Who's going to hold you on the day that you die?
Who's going to kiss your neck?
Are my parents on the other side?
Wooo wooo

Chorus

Knew you couldn't lose.

Chords:
Key of D
D em D A
D em bm

There's Time for That

March 4, 2018

Time to go to bed.
You need to rest your head.
Time for you to sleep.
You do need to dream.

You're going to miss that show.
Others will let you know.
School's an early day.
Time to hit the hay.

So, you want to grow up fast,
be like the big kids at last,
stay up late, go on a date.
Hey hesitate
There's time for that.
There's time for that.

Getting old ain't what it seems.
Bills can sink your dreams.
Time for you to learn.
Plenty of time to earn.

So, you want to grow up fast,
be like the big kids at last,
go on that date, stay up late.
Let's hesitate.
There's time for that.
There's time for that.

So, you need to slow it way down
doesn't mean you can't make up ground
just not now, not now

So, close your eyes.
There's a big surprise
of another day.

You get to go out and play.

So, you want to grow up fast,
be like the big kids at last.
So hesitate. It's not too late.
It's gonna last.
There's time for that.
There's time for that.
There's time for that.

Chords:
Capo III Key of C
Am Em Am Em
Am Em Am Em
G Dm G Dm
Am Em Am Em
G Dm G Dm
Chorus:
C G Dm
C G Dm
C G Dm
C G Dm
C G Dm

Leaping into Heaven
March 4, 2018

It's like leaping into heaven
with her children in her arms.
It feels there's nothing better
than to be with those you love.

And the world does spin
and the stars will set.
Our hearts do learn
it's not over yet.

It's like leaping into heaven
when you're in your lover's arms.
Time tends to stand still
when your hearts beat in rhyme.

And the world will spin
and the stars will set;
Our hearts will learn
it's not over yet.

It's like leaping into heaven
the kids at the kitchen table.
Laughter and giggles
telling stories or lost fables.

And world will spin
and the stars set.
Our hearts will learn
it's not over yet.

It's like leaping into heaven
with your daughter in the backseat,
her friends whispering jokes
so easy for my heart to leap.

It's like leaping into heaven
when your boss gives you a raise
and your friends at work
give you lots of praise.

Chords:
Capo III Key of Am
Am C Em G
Am C Em G
Am C Em G
Chorus:
Dm Fmaj7 Am Em
Dm Fmaj7 Am Em

To the Night
February 26, 2018

Wind's up a bit,
blows back her hair,
golden flaxen strands
frame those eyes so fair.

Fire's burning warm,
and the sun is dancing down.
Can't beat back the night
got to give up its daily crown
to the night.

And they do know
that the night will give them
time to talk and touch,
and they do feel
that the night allows
their hearts entwined in love
to be enough.

She squeezes his hands
just to let him know
that he's her man.
She'll never let the cold winds blow.

Fire's burning warm,
and the sun is dancing down.
Can't beat back the night.
Got to give up its daily crown
to the night.

And they do know
that the night will give them
time to talk and touch,
and they do feel
that the night allows
their hearts entwined in love
to be enough.

And they do know
that the night allows the
time to talk and touch,
and they do feel
that the night allows
their hearts entwined in love
to be enough.

Chords:

Capo III Key of Bb
G GAm7 G GAm7 Em7 Am7 G
G GAm7 G GAm7 G GAm7 Em7 Am7 G
Em D5 C B G D5
Em D5 C B G D5
G GAm7 G GAm7 Em7 Am7 G
G GAm7
Am Em D5 C B G D5
Am Em D5 C B G D5
G GAm7 G GAm7 Em7 Am7 G

What's It Going to Take?
February 9, 2018
Written with David J. Skinner and Robb Boyd

Silence cut through dinner.
We all knew it would.
Dad, they're killin' people over there.
Mom pushed back her chair.
Mom pushed back her chair.

What's it going to take
to fill you up?
So many bodies. What's enough?
Body count's up.
Body count's up.

Mother at the door.
Reads a telegram.
She can't give more.
She now gives a damn.
She now gives a damn.

What's it going to take
to fill you up?
So many bodies. What's enough?
Body count's up.
Body count's up.

Was it a lie that brought you here?
and that lie we all fear?

Body count's up.
Body count's up.

They lined up at the mall,
Protesters wall to wall.
Politicians wouldn't pay attention
or listen at all,
or listen at all.

What's it going to take
to fill you up?
So many bodies. What's enough?
Body count's up.
Body count's up.

Chords:
Key of G
G D Em7 C
G D Em7 C
G D Em7 C
G D Em7 C
Bm C Am D5
Bm C Am D5

I'll Never Be the Same
February 9, 2018
Written with David J. Skinner

She's just an angel walking away.
Seems like she's floating above the fray.
I'll never be the same.
I'll never be the same.

She's just that girl at the coffee shop,
turned and smiled, and my heart did stop.
I'll never be the same.
I'll never be the same.

And the moon did show tonight
and my chance at love seemed so right.
So, come on moon, glow bright.
I'll never be the same.
I'll never be the same.
I'll never be the same.

I'll never be the same.
I'll never be the same.

And the moon did show tonight.
My chance at love seemed so right.
So, come on moon, glow bright.
I'll never be the same.
I'll never be the same.
I'll never be the same.

Chords:
Capo III
D5 Em11
D5 Em11
B C#
B C#
D5 Em11
D5 Em11
B C#
B C3
Bm A G
Bm A G
Bm A G
Bb6 B C#
B C#

Capo III
D9
B C# D9
B C# D9

D9
B C# D9
B C# D9

Bm A G
Bm A G
Bm A G

The Sun Rises

February 8, 2018

She sure is pretty. She sure is sweet.
On the plane flying, across the sea.
And the sun rises, oh, the sun rises in my heart.

Chorus:
Been too long waiting, too much time between.
Distance is hard, but he knows, oh, he knows.
The sun rises, oh, the sun rises in his heart.

Life can be messy, life can be tough.
It's worth living. Don't give up.
The sun rises, oh, the sun rises in your heart.

Chorus

Some say your chances are over and done.
Don't listen to them. You'll find your one.
For the sun rises, oh, the sun rises in your heart.

Chorus

Chorus

Chords:
Capo III
G D Em
G D Em
Am B C
Am B C
G D Em
G D Dm
D9 Em C G

D9 Em C G
Am B C
Am B C

Can He Care?
January 27, 2018

Can he care?
Can he love?
Is his heart fractured and broken,
his life just a token spent like a wallet lent out?

Can he give, much less live?
His feelings just empty shouts
like the rain running down the spout
deep in the earth and out of sight.

He's gonna love. He's gonna give.
Once he finds his woman, he'll live.

For he needs to be the man he wishes
Needs to be the man he wishes

Can he lead, fill their needs?
His life was battered and torn,
his needs scattered and torn
across the empty sea.
Wants to know who he can be.

He's gonna love. He's gonna give.
Once he finds his woman he'll live.

For his heart is strong. His life's not wrong.
He's been searching his whole life long.

He can care.
He will love.
For his heart is not fractured or broken,
and his love is not a token spent on love
not earned.
His life's not here, and he's been burned.

Chords:
Capo III
Em D/G G
Em D/G G
Am D9 Bm C walk down
C G D9
C G D9

Hop a Plane
January 18, 2018

She's got that body and mind.
Going to drive him crazy.
Her life and art's divine.
He won't say maybe.

He's going to find some time
to hop a plane.
Going to go across that sea
to get her to change her name.

When he spends time there
and sees her art
just hanging on those walls,
he doesn't want to be apart

He's going to find some time
to hop a plane.
Going to go across that sea
to get her to change her name.
Going to go across that sea
to get her to change her name.

He's had his sorrow
and too much pain.
She brings him laughter.
He'll never be the same.

He's going to make some time
to hop a plane.
Want to go across that sea
Got to go across that sea
Want to go across that sea
and get her to change her name.
Going to go across that sea
and get her to change her name.

She's got that body and mind
going to drive him crazy.
His life and art's divine.
He won't get lazy.
His life and art's divine.
He won't get lazy.
His life and art's divine.
He won't get lazy.

Chords:
Capo II Key of Bb
G D/F# Em7
G D/F# Em7
Chorus:
C G C D
G D/F# Em C Am D

Driving in a Whiteout
January 10, 2018

Chorus:
He's driving in a whiteout, and it's hard.
Can't see in front or behind. It's just getting dark.
Getting dark.

She didn't answer the phone when he called.
She doesn't seem to be at the mall.
He doesn't know what's her deal.
Is she for real?

Chorus

Gotta go home.
She left a note on the door.
She can't see him no more.
It's time to move on.
She said, "So long."

His life is in a whiteout, and it's hard.
Can't see in front or behind. He's just in the dark.
He's just in the dark.

Chorus

Getting dark.
He keeps fighting the snow.
Wants to know which way to go.
The cold weather in his heart
kept him apart.

His life is in a whiteout, and it's hard.
Can't see in front or behind. Just gettin' dark.
Just gettin' dark.

Chorus

Just getting dark.
Just getting dark.

Chords:
Capo IV Key of G
G Am7 Am/C Am G
G Am7 Am/C Am G
Am7 Am/C Bm/F# Cadd9 Bm/F# Cadd9
Chorus:
Em7 F#7#5 G CmajAdd9
Em7 F#7#5 G CmajAdd9
G Cmajadd9
G Cmajadd9 walk down 2x

I Got on a Plane: Songs of 2017

The song "I Got on a Plane" was written at the Four Seasons
Hotel in Chicago after I came back from Edinburgh and Berlin.
Such a fun song. I first introduced it to the public at The Bluebird
Café in Nashville in August of 2017, courtesy of Steve Leslie.
"Whiskey Is Warm" came to me after a work event at the Iron
Fish Distillery, just outside of Traverse City, Michigan. I wrote
"A Song for Susan" for my best friend's wife.

Island Christmas
December 30, 2017
Islamorada, Florida

Come to the island. It's Christmas time.
Come to the island and have the time of your life.

Chorus:
Cause we got
Christmas trees in the sand,
mermaids and
turtles that swim (roll)/3rd dolphins that smile

Come to the island for the wind and the waves.
Come to the island
Some say it may
save your soul

Chorus

Break

You won't want to go home 'cause it just won't snow
So, come on stay a month
Come to the island. It's Christmas time.
We're here to serve you, so leave your troubles behind.

Chorus

Come to the island it's Christmas time
You'll have the time of your life we know
Come and it won't snow

Chorus

Come to the island. it's Christmas time.
Come to the island.
You'll have the time of your life.
I always wanted to live on the island.
But I just can't now.

Come to the island. It's Christmas time.
You'll have the time of your life we know,
'cause it won't snow

Chorus

Come to the island. It's Christmas time.
Come to the island. It's Christmas time.
Come to the island. It's Christmas time.

Chords:

Capo II Key of B

A A6th Amaj7 A6th

A A6th Amaj7 A6th

Esus4 E

Chorus:

F#m F#mMaj7 F#/Em7 Esus4 E

Break:

D E Asus2 F#m Bm Esus4 E

Whiskey Is Warm
November 3, 2017

They lined 'em up in a row,
poured 'em deep and poured them slow.
His heart was crushed tonight,
another evening fighting his fight.

Chorus:
Too often he's in the bottle
seeking shelter from the storm.
Winters are long, and whiskey is warm.
Oh, it's warm, warm, warm.

All his life he's lived alone.
Felt this girl was his home.
She turned and walked away.
He's fighting that fight even today.

Chorus

Break (Boo-doo-doo, etc.)

Chorus

The job was over last month.
Landlord has had enough.
Needs a place to stay.
Choices he's made has had him pay.

Chorus

He hit bottom the other day.
Joined a group to change his ways.
They lined 'em up in a row.
He turned around and let them go

Chorus

Chorus

Chords:
Capo II Key of G
Em C Em C
Em C Em C
D C D C
C G Am C G Bm7
C G Am Bm7 C

I'll Never Stop Falling in Love
October 27, 2017

He was my provider, and the father
of my little ones.
Gave me safety and security,
when day was done.

I'll never stop falling in love
Fall in love with you
I'll never stop falling in love
Fall in love with you

My world was a wreck before I met you.
We had a life.
Taught me family is important.
Dinner on Sunday night.

I'll never stop falling in love
Fall in love with you
I'll never stop falling in love
Fall in love with you

I'll never stop falling in love
Fall in love with you
I'll never stop falling in love
Fall in love with you

No need to find another
'cause he's the one.
Handsome and strong I knew
I was the lucky one.

I'll never stop falling in love
Fall in love with you
I'll never stop falling in love
Fall in love with you

I'll never stop falling in love
Fall in love with you
I'll never stop falling in love
Fall in love with you

Chords:

Capo IV Key of E
Am G6add9 F#min7flat13th Fmaj7
Am G6add9 Am
Am G6add9 F#min7flat13th Fmaj7
Am G6add9 Am

C G C/Emaj7 Fmaj7 FM#11 Fmaj7 FM#11
C G C/Emaj7 Fmaj7 FM#11 Fmaj7 FM#11

The Day You Were Born
September 27, 2017
(Tempo: 98)

God sang the day you were born.
Angels lined up in rows
and played their horns.

Wanna say, "Glad you're here."
There're angels dancing in your hair.

God laughed the day you were born
gave you the gift of humor I knew it was yours.

Wanna say,"Glad you're here."
Wanna know that you're near.
Are those angels dancing in your hair?

God danced the day you were born,
did the two-step and spun the floor.

Wanna say, "Glad you're here."
Wanna feel that you're near.
Are those angels dancing in your hair?

Wanna say, "Glad you're here."
Wanna feel that you're near
with those angels dancing in your hair.

God smiled the day you were born.
Bells were ringing from night till morn.

Wanna say, "Glad you're here."
There're angels dancing in your hair.

God sang the day you were born.
Angels lined up in rows and blew their horns.

Wanna say, "Glad you're here."
Wanna feel that you're near
with those angels dancing in your hair,
those angels dancing in your hair.

Wanna say, "Glad you're here."
Wanna feel that you're near
with those angels dancing in your hair.

Chords:
Capo IV
C G Emaddb5 Em F
C G Emaddb5 Em F
Emaddb5 Em F Am G F
Emaddb5 Em F Am G F
Am G

Cassini Bound
September 21, 2017

Though the moons of Saturn are plenty
and my heart is broken, so mend me
I need you tonight
Like a satellite needs to fly

Chorus 1:
She's crashing through the rings
Gathering speed, headed to ground
My heart and love are Cassini bound

And we seem to miss our orbit
and my rocket's empty, it's over
I wanted you forever
So, I'll just look to the sky

Chorus 2:
She's ripping through the rings
Gathering speed, tearing towards ground
And my heart and love
And my heart and love are Cassini bound

Chorus 2

And my ship needs repair
and the dock is empty, who cares?
I needed you tonight
Like a satellite needs to spin

Chorus 2

Chords:

Capo II Key of G

G Em/G G Em/G

G Em/G G Em/G

Am F#m7#5 Bm11/F# G6 Gmaj

Am F#m7#5 G F# Em G F# Em

Am ABminadd2nd C

If I Could Walk Away
September 2, 2017

The cards aren't in it
The dice can't win it
My luck with you

My heart's been waiting
your board's been taken
This game with you

Chorus:
If I could walk away
I'd head to your town
Though your walls are up
I'll bring 'em down

Soul's been aching
Heart's been breakin'
this life with you

Our date was broken
your tune's been spoken
My song with you

Chorus

Your pawn's been knighted
my king's been sighted
checkmate from you

If I could walk away
I'd walk straight to you
The songs I write are soft and true

If I could walk away
I'd walk straight to you
The songbird tells me
my song with you is thru

The cards aren't in it
my heart can't win it
My loss of you

The cards aren't in it
my heart can't win it
time to leave you

If I could walk away
I'd head out of town
My songbird tells me
time to find new ground

My heart's not in it
Heart's not in it

My heart's not in it
My heart's not in it

Chords:
Capo II Key of D
D5th D6th omit 3rd D5th D6th omit 3rd
Bm7 A Gmaj
D5th D6th omit 3rd D5th D6th omit 3rd
Bm7 A Gmaj
Chorus:
A Bm Gmaj
A Bm Gmaj

A Song for Susan
August 24, 2017

I've known this lady most my life
My best friend's wonderful wife
She helps many in need
She can help them succeed

She's so generous
and I think fabulous
Did I say remarkable
and oh, so talkable
She can work a room

She's a librarian by trade
an educator, the lives she's changed
she helps many in need
she can help them succeed

She's so generous
and I think fabulous
Did I say remarkable
and oh, so talkable
She can work a room

I've known this lady most my life
my best friend's wonderful wife
She helps many in need
She can help them succeed

Did I say generous
Did I say fabulous
Did I say remarkable
and oh, so talkable
She can work a room

I've known this lady most my life

Chords:

Capo III

D C G6thsus 2nd G5th add 9th b 11th

D C G6thsus 2nd G5th add 9th b 11th

D C G6thsus 2nd G5th add 9th b 11th

D C G6thsus 2nd G5th add 9th b 11th

D C Am7 G6thsus 2nd G5th add 9th b 11th

D C Am7 G6thsus 2nd G5th add 9th b 11th

C Am7 D G Em

C Am7 D G Em

G F# Em

Am7 G6thsus 2nd G5th add 9th b 11th

D C Am7 G6thsus 2nd G5th add 9th b 11th

I Had Two Mothers
August 19, 2017

I had two mothers raised me up
one lived long and the other died young
She was Cherokee and half black
Her husband helped me be the man I am

I love them and miss them so much
They helped me to be tough

It's the love you have and the love you need
Open your heart it's safe to believe
It's the connections you keep that helps you to live
She taught me to love, and she taught me to give

I worked in a shop
where we shined those shoes
the friends I made, I'll never lose
I love them and miss them so much
They helped me to be leather tough

It's the love you have and the love you need
Open your heart it's safe to believe
It's the connections you keep that help you to live
She taught me to love and she taught me to forgive

I helped them build their home on the corner
by the park where we would gather
on Sunday mornings we all would meet
They helped so many stay off the street

I miss them and love them so much
They helped me to be leather tough

It's the love you have and the love that you need
Open your heart it's safe to believe
It's the connections you keep that helps you to live
She taught me to love and she taught me to forgive

I had two mothers raised me up
One lived long and the other died way too young

Chords:
Capo V Key of G
G G/F# maj 7th G/E 6th
G G/F# maj 7th G/E 6th
G G/F# maj 7th G/E 6th
G G/F# maj 7th G/E 6th
C C/B maj 7th Am7 Am7/G
C C/B maj 7th Am7 Am7/G
G G/F# maj 7th G/E 6th
G G/F# maj 7th G/E 6th

G F#min 7th sharp 5th Em C
G F#min 7th sharp 5th Em C
G F#min 7th sharp 5th Em C
G F#min 7th sharp 5th Em C

I Got on a Plane
July 29, 2017

Oh, the sun will rise
and the moon will set
I'm thinking I
haven't got her yet

I got on a plane
I traveled across the world
2,000 miles
Just to meet this girl

The wind will blow
and the trees will shake
I couldn't know
What it's going to take

I got on a plane
I traveled across the world
2,000 miles
Just to meet this girl

The leaves will fall
and weather change
I sense it's coming
Will she be the same?

I got on a plane
I traveled across the world
2,000 miles
Just to meet this girl

I got on a plane
I traveled across the world
2,000 miles
Just to get that girl

The moon will rise
and the sun will set
I'm thinking I'm
Gonna get her yet

I took a plane
I traveled across the world
2,000 miles
Just to get this girl
Just to get this girl
Just to get this girl

Chords:
Capo V
Am CM13/B C
Am CM13/B Am
Am Cm13/B C
Am Cm13/B

F Em Am
F Em Am
F Em Am
F G Am CM13/B D

What He'd Do for You
July 12, 2017

He's been looking
Just last love searching
Now he knows
You're on that road with him

What he'd do for you
He'd walk around the moon
Swim oceans wide
Just to be by your side

He's so grateful
He can't be hateful
Now he holds
Time for you tonight

What he'd do for you
He'd circle the moon
Swim oceans wide
Just to be by your side

Now he knows
You're on that road with him

What he'd do for you
He'd trek across the moon

Swim oceans wide
Just to be by your side

He's been looking
with great luck searching
Now he's found
you to share his life

What he'd do for you
He'd crawl across the moon
Swim oceans wide
Just to be by your side

What he'd do for you
He'd swim across the moon
Walk oceans wide
Just to be by your side

Chords:
Capo III
C Csus2 Fmaj7 FM#11sus2
C Csus2 Fmaj7 FM#11sus2
C A9sus4th Am A9sus4th F Am
G A B C B
G A B C B

Am F G
G A B C
Am F G
G A B C
Am F Am F
G A B C B
G A B C B

Raw Sugar
July 8, 2017

She walks into the room
Everyone turns their head
She moves oh so smooth
At least that's what the ladies said

'Cause she's got that raw sugar
She sweetens everyone she meets
She's got that raw sugar
Raw sugar
Raw sugar
Raw sugar

She came from another land
Came here just for love
She's looking for her man
Not sure where he's coming from

'Cause she's got that raw sugar
Raw sugar sweetens me
She's got that raw sugar
Raw sugar
Raw sugar
Raw sugar sweetens me

He asked for an introduction
She said no
Wasn't looking for seduction
Wasn't gonna go down that road

'Cause she comes with raw sugar
She sweetens everything she does
She's got that raw sugar
Raw sugar
Raw sugar

Raw sugar sweetens me
Raw sugar

She walks into the room
Everyone moves their head
She moves oh so smooth
At least that's what he said

'Cause she comes with raw sugar
She sweetens everything she does
She's got that raw sugar
Raw sugar
Raw sugar
Raw sugar, come sweeten me
Raw sugar, come sweeten me

She comes with raw sugar
She sweetens everything she does
She's got that raw sugar
Raw sugar
Raw sugar
Raw sugar, come sweeten me
Raw sugar, come sweeten me
Raw sugar

Chords:
Capo III
Am F#7sus4#5 G6 F#7sus4#5
Am Am/C Asus2/B E
Am F#7sus4#5 G6 F#7sus4#5
Am Am/C Asus2/B E

F G Am7 Am/C
F G Em Am
F G Am7 Am/C
F G Em Am
F G Em Am
F G Em Am
F G F

Leave Your Love Behind
April 7, 2017

He's gonna leave your love behind
Heart says time to go
His friends say don't
Others say he won't

It's time for him to move on
So long
Time to write another song
So sorry took your time
Goodbye
Time to write another rhyme
Goodbye

It's been fun, and you're so cool
Somehow, he felt the fool
So, it's begun
His walk now is a run

It's time for him to move on
So long
Time to write another song
So sorry took your time
Goodbye
Time to write another rhyme
Goodbye

Time and distance makes it tough
Long distance love is rough
So, it's begun
and you aren't the one

He's gonna take his time
Goodbye
Time to write another rhyme
It's time for him to move on
So long
Time to write another song
So long
So long
So long
So long

Chords:
Capo III (G form) Key of A
G Em G Em
C G C G
Chorus:
D Em C
G C
D Em C
G

Met This Woman
March 29, 2017

Met this woman, met this lady, met this love
Someone he wants to know more of
She is laughter, she is substance and time
Someone to complete his rhyme

Grab your pack, hop this plane
Got to go
Squeeze a life into three days
Take your guitar, write a song
Don't you know
Airports take their toll

Met a beauty, met an angel from above
Someone he wants to know more of
She is sunshine, she is moonshine and wind
Blowing up and down no end

Grab your bag, hop this plane
Got to go
Make a life in three days
Take your guitar, sing a song
And it shows
As your joy unfolds

He met this woman, met this lady, met his love
Someone he can't live without
She is laughter, she is sunshine and wind
Their life together begins

So, grab your bag, hop this plane
Let's go
We'll make a life in three days
I've got my guitar, all I need is
you to show
We'll head to where it don't snow

So, meet this woman, meet this lady, meet his love
It's all he ever thinks of
She is laughter, she is sunshine and wind
Their life together won't end

So, grab your heart, pack your bag
Let's go
We've got more than three days
I've got my guitar, all I need is you
The weather there is great

Chords:
Capo III Key of F (D form)
D5th Em11th F#min#5th add flat 2nd Bm7th#5
D5th Bm7th#5 A Asus4th A
D5th Em11th F#min#5th add flat 2nd Bm7th#5
D5th Bm7th#5 Asus4th

G D/F#maj Em D/F#maj G D/F#maj Asus4th
G D/F#maj Em D/F#maj G D/F#maj Asus4th

The American Dream
February 27, 2017

They left their homeland for the States
with a baby in tow, a spouse who didn't know
the language oh, how could they dare
leave their home with nothing to spare?

With effort they found work
new friends helped them out
a place to stay, they got out

It's just a chance at the American Dream
Get up early, you know what it means
The American Dream

Work hard, get your card, and show up
Teach your children it's time to grow up
They love this land
Let freedom stand

Cause it's just a chance at the American Dream
Get up early, they know what it means
the American Dream

They raised a family and did their part
Learned to take some risk
Many failed, some would hit

It's just a chance at the American Dream
Get up early, you know, what it means
The American Dream
The American Dream

Work hard, become a citizen
and show up
teach your children it's time to grow up

They love this land
Let freedom stand

Cause it's just a chance at the American Dream
Get up early, I know what it means
It's the American Dream

It's just a chance at the American Dream
Get up early, we know what it means
It's the American Dream
It's the American Dream

Chords:
Capo II
Am FM7#5 Am FM7#5
Am FM7#5 Am FM7#5
F Em F Em
C walk down
Fmaj7 G11/F C walk down
Fmaj7 G11/F
Chorus:
C walk down
Fmaj7 G11/F C walk down
Fmaj7 G11/F
Em F Am G
Em F Am G
F Em F Em
C walk down
Fmaj7 G11/F C walk down
Fmaj7 G11/F

About the Songwriter

Daniel S. Terry started writing guitar music as a youth in Kewanee, Illinois after his sister gave him a discarded guitar. He bought a tuning fork, a Beatles' chord book and taught himself how to play. He first wrote songs with a friend. At 13, after his mother died, he wrote his first solo song, "She Is Gone." Later, he was part of a high school folk rock band called "The Tangerine Doorknobs." He played and wrote original songs during college and grad school, and then took a creative break for 25 years.

In late 2015, Terry began composing and writing songs again daily – at home, on the road, in airports, hotels, parks, and cities around the world. He travels with a Taylor GS Mini Koa wood guitar. Terry completes and records about 20 new songs a year. Learn more on his web site DanielSTerrySongs.com.

Look for his professional music videos with actors and a Nashville backup band on his YouTube channel, Daniel S Terry. Follow the latest compositions, song thoughts and events on Facebook (@DanTerrySongs) and Instagram (@DanT18605).

Index

A

American Dream, 121, 122, 129
angel, 3, 4, 83, 119
art, 89, 90

B

birds, 45
birthdays, 41
Boyd, Robb, 81
by my side, 39

C

cards, 105, 106
care, 2, 15, 53, 87
cared, 27, 28
Cassini, 103, 128
Christmas, 94, 95, 128
city, 19
comets, 27
connections, 109

D

dad, 53
dance, 45, 63, 67
dancing, 79, 101, 102
dark, 91, 92
death, 57
die, 73, 74
died, viii, 56, 109, 110, 123
dream, 75

F

family, viii, 21, 63, 99, 121
fate, 23
father, 33, 53, 99
fight, 71, 97
fresh start, 1
friends, 11, 19, 21, 56, 73, 77, 78, 109, 117, 121

G

game, 105

give, 17, 18, 33, 38, 39, 60, 78, 79, 81, 85, 87, 109
go back, 19
goodbye, 117, 118
grateful, 33, 113
guitar, viii, 25, 26, 119, 120, 123

H

heart, i, ii, viii, 3, 6, 7, 9, 17, 18, 19, 20, 27, 33, 35, 37, 38, 47, 49, 50, 51, 60, 63, 67, 74, 77, 83, 85, 87, 91, 97, 103, 105, 106, 109, 117, 120, 128, 129
hearts, 38, 60, 63, 67, 77, 79, 80
heaven, 21, 22, 44, 77, 78
help, 7, 43, 44, 51, 107, 109
home, 6, 15, 16, 23, 51, 60, 91, 95, 97, 109, 121, 123
husband, 41, 42, 109

I

in my arms, 3, 47, 49
island, 94, 95

J

joy, 17, 18, 65, 67, 119

K

kind, 9, 17, 27, 35
kiss, 39, 71, 73, 74

L

laugh, 17, 18, 63
laughter, 62, 67, 73, 89, 119, 120
left, viii, 13, 29, 30, 91, 121
Leslie, Steve, viii, 94
life, viii, 1, 11, 19, 21, 29, 31, 33, 38, 39, 41, 42, 44, 47, 56, 59, 62, 63, 67, 71, 85, 87, 89, 90, 91, 94, 95, 97, 99, 105, 107, 113, 119, 120, 128, 129
lonely, 13
loss, 106
love, iii, 3, 7, 9, 11, 13, 17, 18, 21, 23, 29, 31, 33, 35, 37, 38, 41, 42, 44, 45, 47, 49, 51, 55, 60, 65, 67, 69, 73, 77, 79, 80, 83, 87, 99, 100, 103, 109, 113, 115, 117, 119, 120, 121
loved, 13, 23, 27, 28, 33, 51, 67, 73, 74
lover, 13, 77
lovers, 31, 43

M

man, 23, 35, 36, 51, 53, 57, 60, 73, 79, 87, 109, 115

missing, 19, 20
mistress, 65
mom, 15, 81
moon, 27, 39, 47, 83, 111, 112, 113, 114
mother, viii, 33, 81, 123
mothers, 109, 110
move on, 1, 27, 91, 117, 118
music, ii, viii, 6, 18, 37, 59, 65, 123

N

new day, 56, 57
night, 21, 33, 38, 57, 65, 79, 80, 99, 101

O

oceans, 51, 67, 113, 114

P

packed, 23, 29
park, 25, 26, 109
plane, 85, 89, 111, 112, 119

R

remember
    couldn't remember, 37, 41, 129
road, 13, 59, 63, 113, 115, 123

S

saint, 29, 31
sand, 25, 26, 31, 73, 94
Saturn, 103
sea, 51, 85, 87, 89
seasons, 9, 47, 62
ship, 103
sing, viii, 33, 45, 56, 63, 71, 73, 119
single mom, 55
Skinner, David J., 81, 83
sky, 25, 26, 37, 49, 103
sleep, 57, 75
smile, 17, 56, 57, 62, 94
snow, 9, 13, 25, 45, 91, 95, 119
song, iii, viii, 1, 17, 18, 33, 37, 57, 65, 71, 94, 105, 117, 118, 119, 123
spring, 69
stars, 25, 26, 33, 77
stay, 67
summer, 6, 25, 26, 129

sun, 9, 25, 26, 37, 39, 47, 57, 62, 67, 79, 85, 111, 112
sunshine, 119, 120
Susan, 94, 107, 128

T

tears, 13, 55, 56, 57
TenBrink, Rebecca, 1
the day you were born, 101, 102
time, 1, 2, 6, 9, 11, 17, 18, 27, 29, 38, 47, 49, 51, 53, 56, 57, 60, 63, 75, 76, 79, 80, 85, 89, 91, 94, 95, 106, 117, 118, 119, 121
toast, 56
tonight, 67, 71, 83, 97, 103, 113

W

walk away, 105, 106
weather, 91, 111, 120
whiteout, 91
widow, 51
wife, 11, 63, 71, 94, 107
wind, 23, 25, 26, 41, 49, 59, 95, 111, 119, 120
winter, 25
woman, 62, 87, 119, 120
work, 11, 12, 17, 29, 43, 69, 71, 78, 94, 107, 121
world, viii, 77, 99, 111, 112, 123

Y

years, iii, viii, 13, 32, 37, 41, 42, 55, 71, 123

Z

Zuzelski, Emily, 13, 15, 17

Alphabetical Listing of Songs

Song	**Page**
A Song for Susan	107
A Woman in His Life	62
Big City Lights	19
Can He Care?	87
Can Love Grab Hold	9
Can't Stop, Won't Stop	45
Cassini Bound	103
Diamond in the Rough	69
Don't Light the Torch	15
Driving in a Whiteout	91
Enough of This Fight	71
Every Saint	31
Every Storm	35
Gold Digger	27
Grateful for Love	33
Heads or Tails	23
Heart Tones	37
Hop a Plane	89
How Do You Get	11
I Got on a Plane	111
I Had Two Mothers	109
If I Could Walk Away	105
I'll Never Be the Same	83
I'll Never Stop Falling in Love	99
In My Arms	3
Island Christmas	94
It's Gonna Get Better	6
I've Got a Plan for Heaven	21
Leaping into Heaven	77
Leave Your Love Behind	117
Met This Woman	119
Mistress	65

Move On	1
My Dad	53
My Life Is Better with You	39
Out of Time	47
Raw Sugar	115
She Couldn't Remember	41
Summer's Here	25
Take a Chance on Our Dance	67
The American Dream	121
The Day You Were Born	101
The Girl from Jericho	13
The Human Heart	17
The Only Way Is Up	55
The Sky Is Crying	49
The Sun Rises	85
There's a New Day Coming	56
There's Time for That	75
Through the Glass	29
To the Night	79
What He'd Do for You	113
What's It Going to Take?	81
When She Loves	59
Which Way to Go	63
Whiskey Is Warm	97
Who's Going to Sing to You?	73
Who's Got Your Back	43
Widow of the Oceans	51

Made in the USA
Monee, IL
21 August 2021